Robert Loudoun

Songs of Venice

And Other Poems

Robert Loudoun

Songs of Venice
And Other Poems

ISBN/EAN: 9783744717229

Printed in Europe, USA, Canada, Australia, Japan

Cover: Foto ©Thomas Meinert / pixelio.de

More available books at **www.hansebooks.com**

SONGS OF VENICE.

AND OTHER POEMS

BY

ROBERT LOUDOUN.

And I have said and I say it ever,
As the years go on and the world goes over,
'Twere better to be content and clever
In tending of cattle and tossing of clover,
In the grazing of cattle and the growing of grain,
Than a strong man striving for wealth and gain;
Be even as kine in the red-tipped clover,
For they lie down and their rests are rests.
—ARIZONIAN.

CLEVELAND, O:
WILLIAM W. WILLIAMS,
MDCCCLXXXV.

CONTENTS.

	PAGE.
PRELUDE.	
SONGS OF VENICE:	
The Serenade	13
The Dream	18
A Reverie	21
The Gondolier	24
Thou Bride of the Ocean	27
She Sleeps Upon the Sea	28
Sibylline	30
POEMS OF LOVE:	
Anna Belle	36
Daphne	39
I Would be Free	50
The Fountain of Youth	52
'Neath the Willows	55
Drifting	60
A Portrait	63
Longing	65
A Greeting From the South	68
Birds of Night	70
Faded Roses	74

CONTENTS.

SONNETS:

	PAGE.
Hope	79
Hellas	80
Hellas	81
Hellas	82
Aphrodite	83
Virginia	84
Virginia	85
Montecello	86
Chippewa	87
Chippewa	88
Chippewa	89
Salutation	90
Constancy	91
A Tribute	92
You Bid Me Sing	93
The Past	94
Beauty	95
Resolution	96
Hebe	97
Hebe	98
No Love is Lost	99
Love Immortal	100
Emerson	101
Moiræ	102
Youth's Love	103
Flight of Years	104
Epigram	105
Apollo Scorned	106

CONTENTS.

PAGE.

SYLVAN:

- Elywood 109
- Gathering Arbutus 116
- The Advent of Summer 122
- The Poet's Path 123
- Nature's Freedom 125
- Morn 127
- Nature Healeth 130
- Light 134

OCCASIONAL PIECES:

- Titus Livius—A Requiem 139
- Ambition 145
- The Fallen 146
- Alice 151
- Memorial Day 154
- Byron 157
- Banquet Song 159
- Normia 161
- Thanksgiving 163
- The Fate of Tasso 165

PRELUDE.

If in this early flight of tuneless song
I leave the beaten track, where oft and long,
The feet of countless pilgrims trod before,
And roam through meadows, by the shadowy shore
Of woodland streams, o'erarched by lacing limbs,
That e'en in midday fiercest sunlight dims;
Where cattle stray in low, cool alder swamps,
Drinking from weird and willowed river-damps;
By mountain tarns and their steep cataracts
Far-hiding where no vulgar eye attracts;
In caverned rocks, deep-sounding to the tread,
Where Echo leads, forgetful of all dread
Mysterious sounds that follow in her way,—
Till lost, bewilder'd, far from genial day,
I fain would hasten to the light again,
Content to walk by down and reedy fen,—
Seeking no more the mysteries that woo
The curious mind away from nature true
But to perplex and taint with vague distrust,

The free-born spirit that would 'scape its rust,
And sing in simple song the thoughts that rise
From feeling deep or forms that charm the eyes—
Perchance a handful of wild flowers I'll gather,
Heedless of color, perfume, odor: rather,
A mingled chain of daffodils and clover,
Chosen at random by a thoughtless rover,
In idle moments loitering through the fields
In summer weather, caring for naught that yields
More than the pleasure of the passing hour
And twilight skies that call him to love's bower.

I would not more; ambition's siren voice
Falls harsh and hollow with no charm or choice,
But hither go where fancy leads the way
Though all condemn my wanton minstrelsy.

Songs of Venice.

THE SERENADE.

>'Tis sweet to hear
>At midnight on the blue and moonlit deep
>The song and oar of Adria's gondolier,
>By distance mellowed o'er the water's sweep.
>
>—*Don Juan, Can. I.*

'Twas the midnight's soft hour, and the silence of Venice
Unbroke was by tumult, the sounds that dismiss
From the mind its soft musings that flow on like a river,
Unchecked in its channel in beauty forever;
While each bend and each sway in the course it pursues
Gives new pleasure, new transport, new beauties it strews
'Long the fens that we follow.
     'Twas the midnight's soft hour;
Far away in dark Santa Maria's high tower
The bell tolled for mass, and the monk counted low
His beads in dull silence: the chants' solemn flow

Disturbed not his prayers, for the shades down in Hades
Were as far from his thoughts as the damsels of Cadiz.
The lights at long intervals gleamed on the water
But palely, for through the deep sky ever brighter,
The stars shone, and moon in its fair waxing crescent,
Silvered turret and temple and palace and casement
With strange light. The splash of a light guarded oar
Alone broke the stillness the bells broke before—
But had ceased—as the boat softly stole through the shade
Unreached by the moonlight that sought to invade,
And near now approached to the place where his love
Slept in beauty: unknown was the passion which strove
In the breast of the gallant who glided beneath
Her high, open window. The last carnival wreath
Still hung from the balcony, drooping and sere,
Where soft hands had pressed it in leaning more near

To the bright laughing throng in their close crowded
    boats,
Filled with youth and with pleasure.
                                Now softly the notes
Of his prelude responded the touch of his fingers,
As expectancy dwells on the music that lingers
A moment behind it, till full on the ear
Blend the voice and the lute-chords, sweet, plaintive
    and clear.

I.

O, fairer far than sirens sleeping
    Upon the silent, waveless ocean,
I know my dearest love now waking,
    In every charm, in every motion;
        Will she not come to me,
        I plead now so earnestly;
Come ere my true heart with fondness is breaking?

II.

Does she not list to the song I'm singing?—
    She dreams in her soft and silken bower,

Will she not heed the love I'm bringing?—
   I sigh for her smile like a drooping flower;
     Can she now refuse it me,
      Know not my heart's sympathy?—
Ah, faintly these chords can tell of its yearning.

III

Shall beauty sleep while love is pining,
   And tells its woes to listless air?
Shall beauty dream while love is chafing,
   Unnoticed by the loved and fair?
     Swiftly I glide away,
     Love disdained cannot stay,
Ah, harsh are the chords when the spirit is sinking.

Scarce had the last sounds of his quivering lute
Died in silence, his soft, pleading voice again mute,
When a white robed figure stole quick to the window
And taking one glance at the gallant below,
Pushed aside with one hand the antique portière,
With the other—her arm, soft, dimpled and bare
Thrust beyond, but in shadow—threw in his boat

A handful of roses; a red one, which smote
His cheek as it passed, her warm lips had pressed:
And the kiss in that moment she gave him unguessed,
Was not wasted, for still in the fragrance he found,
And the touch, soft caressing, more joy than is bound
In roses alone, though from deep Persian skies
Drop the dew on their petals that flash like the eyes
Of the winsomest maidens that wander at eve
Through the palm-groves of Emir.
      He could scarcely conceive
Such fortune was his, such rich Argosies,
In love's own sweet language; and looking up sees
Her white arms, a gleam of her bosom the shade
And the curtain concealed not; a smile that repaid
All his warmest devotion; yet the vision had fled
Ere a moment her beauty his charmed sight had fed.

THE DREAM.

She is dreaming, dreaming sweetly,
   That soft siren of the islands,
On the breast of Italy,
   On her dying fame-washed strands.

See the moon-light gently floating
   O'er the wave and broken walls,
At some gloomy shadow gloating,
   On the Doge's lonely halls.

Silent save the whispering night-wind,
   Creeping 'long the silv'ry streets,
And its murmur soft confin'd
   Where the wall the water meets.

Catch her accents, she is dreaming,
   Yes, again she's with the past,
In the days when fame was streaming
   O'er the seas from every mast.

Now her domes, her gilded steeples,
   With their former lustre shine,
And they dwell—the ancient peoples—
   In this home of beauty's shrine:

When the Orient had yielded
   All the splendor of its arts,
And its gold and pearl had circled
   Pride and pomp in all her marts.

See yon pageant floating proudly,
   Torches gleaming on the waves,
And the people cheering loudly
   Hail it with the captive slaves.

For her warriors now are bringing
   Spoils of victory once more,
And a conquered crown they're flinging
   At her feet, and robes she wore.

Nations all are homage paying
   To this empress of the sea,
And her charms are now subduing
   Each to her own mastery.

And to-night the triumph crowns,
    As her fleet returning home,
Greets them with gay banquet rounds
    'Neath the Doge's palace dome.

They yield, the far-off—but she's waking,
    Dreary, sad and desolate,
Bowing servile to a king,
    Weak, submissive to her fate.

Ah, why should beauty ever be,
    The Nemesis of its own fall,
And humbled pride and heraldry
    Survive alone the death of all?

A REVERIE.

Beneath the portals of Saint Mark I stood—
That wondrous relic of a perished art—
And watched the sun set like a crimson wave
Bathe all the ruins of this noiseless mart
With a new splendor, dim and spirit-like,
Until the city seemed an apparition
Of her dead, lovely self, rising from out
The waveless waters with her ancient pride,
Mocking imagination; as a love
Long lost will haunt our dreams in fairest shape,
And leave us wretched ere the morn has come.

The coast-line waned, then faded from my sight,
And all was dim and formless far and near;
And by and by the great moon rose above
The broken housetops, and once more the streets
Were filled with pleasure-loving, thoughtles throngs:

Light gondolas, and the more stately barge,
And barks with many colored sails that lay
Motionless upon the water, their canvas drooped
About their masts that the still evening stirred not.
And as a I listened, lo, a song broke forth—
A single voice, the words inaudible
By distance, and that mellow tongue that hates
All harshness—soon another caught the strain
And bore it on, and then another answered;
And thus the night wore on, so musical
And sweet, so like her former days of joy,
That for a while I could not but forget
That Venice was a slave, and many stripes
Had bruised her fair, soft shoulders, till the marks
Spoke their own tale of woe, and cried for pity.

A dark robed figure, veiled and lowly bent,
Brushed by me and my dreamy reverie broke.
I watched her enter in and kneel down close
Beside the altar on the cold, bare stone,
And deep sobs shook her bosom as she poured
Her sorrows in the ear of Him who hears
The lowliest, for she had lost her son,

Whom she had loved more than her waning life.
I turned away and felt my eyelids fill,
And like the exiles from fair Babylon
In a strange land, I wept and could not sing;
For I remembered all that she had been,
And never more could be, while time shall last.

THE GONDOLIER.

In Venice Tasso's echoes are no more.
—*Childe Harold Can. IV.*

Can Tasso's songs be silent now?
Me thought the gondolier would vow
Eternal homage to their flow.

Yet, as he guides his graceful bark
Through noiseless streets he sings, but hark!
His thoughts are distant, gloomy, dark.

He sings of Venice in other days;
Her power, her beauty fills his lays,
Nor of his age he tunes the praise.

He sings in snatches, plaintive, low,
Nor merriment his accents know,
Yet music's saddest charm they show.

And like a phantom gliding onward,
How little does his boat accord
With its gay freight and winsome lord.

As floating 'neath the arches crumbling,
And ruined palaces now tumbling
Into the sea with speedy humbling.

Ah, who can tell the sad reflection
Swift-crowding on the mind's dejection,
The softening power of recollection!

For she to him was like a maiden
Whom youth and gayety did gladden,
Nor care nor sorrow ever sadden.

Who dwelt in mirth's seductive rounds,
And followed pace with music's sounds,
Where dance and luxury abounds:

Until o'erpowered with joy and sleep,
And glee no more her revels keep,
She sinks to rest upon the deep.

Ages of glory have passed away,
The gilded boats with color's play,
Yet he alone survives the day,

And in his sable home abides—
'Neath the Rialto still he glides—
The graceful gallant of the tides.

THOU BRIDE OF THE OCEAN.

O, city of Adria's murmuring sea,
What fond recollections cling ever to thee!
  O, sad are the thoughts thy beauty dispelled
  Thou home of the lovely where art long has dwelled!
Still sleep in thy beauty wrapped ever in fame,
O, whisper, breathe gently thy ever loved name—
    Still sleep, sleep gently on—
I sigh not for fortune, the world though it blame,
    I love thee thou bride of the ocean.

SHE SLEEPS UPON THE SEA.

She sleeps, she sleeps upon the sea,
   Beautiful Venice alone,
Dreaming of happy days when free,
   Sighing for pleasures gone.

Hushed are the waves, her pillow light,
   The wind has borne afar—
From Afric's coast, spray gleaming white—
   Upon her silent bar.

In sadness, now, she lightly sleeps,
   Her mantle shorn of beauty,
Her tresses scattered and she weeps
   Lamenting her decree.

SHE SLEEPS UPON THE SEA.

Soft ripples from a distant shore
   Fall lightly at her feet,
Her rest is sacred, and her lore,
   Shines though at setting, sweet.

O, is she weary resting there
   In silent loveliness,
Or is she thinking of the rare
   Fame of her past greatness?

Lone, wrapped in beauteous mystery,
   Nor waking with the day,
She'll ever sleep in her frailty—
   For fled is her life's ray.

SIBYLLINE.

From earliest youth, when first the pictured page
    Chained my young eyes continual,
Thy domes and spires would all my thoughts engage,
    And catch my fancy in their thrall;
Charming the sight like unbound maiden tress
    When gold-hued, glistening in its fall,
Half veiling charms when wanton looks transgress—
    Dream city of unearthly loveliness!

And wert thou like the Cyprian goddess born
    Of sea-foam's softness mid the isles—
Drifting to Italy in the sweet morn—
    And gifted with the secret wiles
That slave all hearts that dare to look on thee,
    With passion's glance, that knows no liberty,
And clings to thy fair palace piles
    As to a love begun in infancy?

What though thy walls are blackened now with time,
    Thy power usurped by foreign hands,
Can aught rob thee of thy own page sublime,
    Thy glory give to other lands?
The heart shall be thy sacred history,
    And fill thy annals with such poesy
As springs from love in its fair prime—
Weaving romance from thy deep mystery.

And if the years deal with unhallowed harshness,
    And the blue sea rise o'er thy ruin,
Thou shalt not lapse into forgetfulness,
    Or future homage fail to win;
To pass from sight is not oblivion
    Save when no worthy deed has e'er been done,
Nor arm been raised amid the din
    Of earth's dissensions, quelling strife begun.

Thy beauty cannot with thy forms decay;
    It is a thing apart from substance,
And will defy time and its sure essay
    To bury all 'neath its advance,

As long as art, romance and poesy
    Shall o'er our minds and hearts hold tender sway;
And when these can no more enhance
    Our lives, 'tis fit that all should pass away.

Poems of Love.

As long as passion has a part in life,
And pride and envy, jealousy and strife,
Usurp the higher instincts of the heart,
In vain no poet sings his humblest part.

Life is illumined by the glow within ;
Love is that light, and rythmic words have been
In every age the noblest form it wears ;
Nor priest, nor creed, such joy the soul e'er bears.

ANNA BELLE.

Bright as the moon-light when it sleeps
    Upon the star-lit, tranquil deep;
Soft as the evening when it creeps
    From shadowy regions of the East;
Fair as the dawn when lingering first
    Upon the topmost mountain peak;
Sweet as the songs that ever burst
    From happy hearts their love thus speak.

A form voluptuous, yet light
    As mist dispelled by morning ray,
And hair that seemed its beauty bright
    Had caught, then lingered there to play
Amid the shower of gold that fell
    Upon her neck of driven snow,
And swelling breast where ever dwell
    In purity, love's warmest glow.

No wild gazelle upon the hills—
   Or bending down with timid grace
Upon the bank of forest rills
   To drink—when it espies the face
Of some lone hunter of the wood
   With levelled gun, never displayed
More eloquence of single look
   Than in her soft blue eyes arrayed.

Languidly beautiful, yet shone
   With all that fascinating charm
Which marked the glance of hers alone,
   The bravest heart they could disarm
If but a single glance were given—
   And at her mercy then it lay—
For Eros had his arrow driven,
   That she with his pierced heart might play.

You should have seen that form where grace,
   In all its beauty seemed to dwell
Immaculate, for that famed race
   In sunny Orient can tell
Of no one fairer when the shades

Of evening gather o'er the wave,
And on the Ganges, India's dusky maids
Come forth, their wondrous forms to lave.

No more you wondering ask me why
My fondest love to her I give,
Or why the passion does not die;
As well attempt, then bid it live,
The fragrance from the rose to separate.

DAPHNE.

Deep in a cool and lone Thesslian wood,
So still and voiceless in its every mood
That contemplation came a guest unbid
And fashioned forms from mortal vision hid;
The god of light and song at evening roved
And woke the measures that his fingers loved,
Since caught by man and fashioned at his will,
To charm all hearts and coldest natures thrill.
    Slow were his steps, for thoughts of deep intent
Seemed fetters in the path his way was bent;
The twittering birds, the startled stags' swift flight
Aroused him not nor claimed his downward sight;
The trampled flowers died sighing to the sound
His wandering fingers heedlessly had found,
Like wind o'er the Æolian strings at night,
Stealing through lattice in a shy affright,
Murmurs weird melody in some high tower

Where Persian maid sleeps in her star-lit bower,
And hears not its complainings while she dreams
Of love and beauty that all real seems;
So he while musing on his mission high—
How he had come from fair Olympus nigh,
To man from gods, and all that he had given
To elevate the mind and heart earth-driven—
To banish ignorance and fill the soul
With perfect light that knows no human goal,
And leaps beyond the confines of dull sense
In realms ideal to find recompense.

His thoughts were of earth's creatures, but no part
Nor portion of them he; in lofty art
And poesy and song, alone he stood
Supreme conservator, and yet he would
That he might win the undying love of her
Whose home was in the ever shadowy river,
Where the Erotas flows through Tempe's vale
Where naught molests or could with harm assail
The sacred muses in their varied rounds
Of mirth and song, while wood and hill resounds
With music wild and choruses led by

Terpsichore, when rays of daylight die
Beyond the purple-wreathèd Cyclades,
And soft delights give pause to stern decrees.
  These Daphne saw when lured from her retreat,
All wondering at the merry, cadenced feet,
And sounds more soft and witching than the shell
Of Nereus in his deep, dark ocean cell,
Wakes for the nymphs.

      One morn before the light
Had risen high, full on his startled sight—
Tripping o'er dew-gemmed flowers—this being came,
But for the moment; ere her sweetest name
The god pronounced, she fled through glist'ning leaves
Of low-hung branches that the vision cleaves
Not; lost she was to his wrapt, eager sight
And ravished heart, and standing in this plight,
Afar he heard her rustling steps away,
Die fainter and still fainter in the gray,
Dull mists of morn.

      Ah, me, how little seemed
His arts divine when she for whom he dreamed

With ceaseless yearning, never moment stayed
When to his eyes her form was once betrayed;
While disappointment kindled that hot fire,
Which, ever burning with renewed desire,
In naught is quenched except satiety—
But such a joy to him could never be.

    In words like these, complaining oft had spoke:
O, Daphne, fairest maid that ever woke
The slumb'ring passion in a god-like heart,
Gladly would I e'er share thy lowly part,
And leave the portals of Elysian light,
If thou stay with me, loveliest earthly sprite—
So shy, evading, vanishing away,
Fleet as the golden shafts of dying day,
When night broods sullenly above the world
And all is shorn of light, in darkness hurl'd;—
So in my soul when thou forsakest me,
Pining, sighing, for thy sweet company.

    But still she would not hear his amorous prayers,
Nor stay her steps, lest falling in the snares
Of love's entanglement, no more returned

She with that peace by maidens higher prized
Than else in life—her perfect chastity;
For Eros had ordained unfeelingly
That she should never know of passion's thrill—
Its swift and fatal thraldom of the will
That yielding once, forever lost restraint
O'er mad desire of which to taste is taint.

          And now this rousèd love unsatisfied,
Intuitive had led him there beside
The stream where fair young Daphne first had given
That deep delight, which since, could know no heaven
But her embrace. Ah! melancholy fate,
That should for this unyielding maid await,
Far from all help, and was there nothing left
But she should be thus of her life bereft?
The god has paused, and list! what melody
Is this that greets his senses? Can it be
Of earth, that one of god-like power should seem
All uncontrolled as waking from a dream?—
A dream in which one clasps a shadow-form,
And kisses lips imaginate, in warm
And wild, impassioned, fancied ecstacy;

Then quickly waking to reality,
Finds bending o'er his couch, gazing the while,
That being who had blessed with sweetest smile
And warm caress, his visioned happiness.
So he when roused from meditativeness,
Dream-like and real to deluded sense,
Found Daphne there—and all the vague suspense
Of love; the image that his mind had wrought
Of her unseen, lay shattered, and seemed naught
Beside her matchless, glowing self incarnate,
While all the air around now seemed vibrate
With melody; sometimes in murmurs lost
Too faint for eager ear though list'ning most
Attentively; sometimes in wild, weird swells,
And echoing like laughter through the dells
Where naiads sport and splash the cooling spray
Of mountain streams in their light, wanton play.
And there she sat upon the shady bank
Close by the river; near and far the rank
Wild flowers grew in sweet profusion, and
These she had gathered, clasped within her hand,
Mingling their fragrance, and their colors twined
Together indiscriminate.   To bind

Her hair—save with the flowers—no thought had
    given,
But framed her face like plumage of the raven,
Falling in ebon coils beyond the curves
Of her small, tapering zone, which naught confines
Now in her still unseen abandonment—
Engaged the while in innocent content.
Fallen was the snowy peplos from the swell
Of her full, maiden breast ; as careless fell
Her form upon the grass ; free were her feet
From sandals, and her limbs seemed fair and fleet
As Dian's when the chase her thoughts engage,
And love knows not her tender vassalage.
Sometimes she bent low to the mirrored stream,
Narcissus like, and saw that heavenly dream
Of love—herself—glassed in the silent surface.
But she knew not that it was beauty, place
Was all to her, and untaught pleasure, joy
That springs, when life knows no alloy
From nature's freedom. Had she known the forms
Shadowed beneath her were the fatal charms
That lured the sun-god to her lone retreat,
Love would have answered beauty, and defeat

Would not have crowned the passion that had driven
His acts to violence, if pitying heaven
Unheeding her, has staid the kindly power
That changed the maid to an undying flower.
Soft: now, while she with arms upraised and hands
Clasped o'er her head; see, through the rippling bands
Of her dark hair, the pearliest shoulders gleam;
The smiles that play upon her red lips seem
Of beauty the perfection; but as free
From passion as the flower that lonely,
Amid the Alpine height's eternal snows,
Blushes and fades though no eye ever knows
Its presence, and no sweet and pure delight
Gives its faint fragrance—for a touch were blight.
All this she saw as swift the placid stream
Mimicked each movement; who could ever deem
She felt no thrill, nor knew the power that dwelt
Within herself, nor all the ill she dealt
Upon her lover most divine.

                                      But hush!
A step steals softly through the grasses lush,
So stealthily, that she with play absorbed

Knew not the god looked on her form disrobed.
And still she heard not till the careless strings
Of his harp, fatal, branch-caught, loudly flings
Its harshest dissonance upon her ear.
O, who could tell the terror, deadly fear,
That held her, though unwilling, to the spot,
And all but her nude loveliness forgot?
She could not flee thus, but her prayer was heard
By her who guardian is, and never barred
Her ears against cries, of dangered chastity:
O, save me! Dian save me! who can stay
The god's strong passion and the rousèd wrath
Stung by disdain of qualities that hath
All minds led captive; for no fault of mine
Has forced me now, this lofty love decline.
What punishment is this that ever closed
The springs of feeling while my beauty soared,
Surpassing mortals, till the envious god
Of love sent this dire vengeance, and has trod
All passion from my heart? I cannot love,
'Tis hateful; though it seems none ever strove
Against this high divinity. Ah, wo

Is me, who cannot this slight gift bestow,
And yielding, stay my fate!

        Thus piteously
She cried, in wild, despairing agony,
And raised on high her supplicating eyes
Pleading relief from the unclouded skies.
Ere the last words had left her pallid lips,
The tender leaves of laurel from the tips
Of her soft fingers, sprang; while from her feet
The grappling roots shot downward as to meet
The earth's moist mold; and what had lately been,
Of all earth-born, more nearly the akin
Of lovely Aphrodite, now assumed
The vernal form that her sweet life entombed
Forever.

     Then, with feelings, deep, intense,
The god made vows that future recompense
All time should pay her, and the leaves henceforth
Should crown alone the man of highest worth.
The scaly trunk then fondly did embrace,
While pitying tear-drops bathed his upturned face,

DAPHNE.

And Daphne wept a fragrant shower of dew
To see the grief that would her fate undo.
Alas! Now saved she was, but martyr still
To modesty and virtue, yet such ill
Were better far than life with shame's hid face
And youth's light merged in dark disgrace.

    Now as I ponder on this story told,
The mist that gathers o'er a fable old
Seems rising, and I read a deeper sense
Hid far beneath this softest color, whence,
The old mythology has often wove
Its tales of passion and undying love.

I WOULD BE FREE.

Turn not on me thy wild, wide eyes,
   I know the magic of their glance,
O, veil thy bosom's gentle rise,
   And free me from this charméd trance!

The night wind never slept so still,
   Nor blossoms breathe such perfume here;
What power is this that chains my will
   And leaves me helpless, thee when near?

Why should I chide my truant heart
   When beauty's face is formed so fair?
The smiles that from thy red lips start,
   Can slave my mind and hold it there.

Touch but thy lips? It cannot be!
   Too deep the thrill, too sweet the joy,
O, tempt me not my vows to flee!
   Such bliss would all my peace destroy.

Turn not on me thy wild, wide eyes,
   For love must follow where they stray;
I would be free as Orient skies,
   From clouds that follow passion's sway.

THE FOUNTAIN OF YOUTH.

*For who hath grieved when soft arms shut him safe,
And all life melted to a happy sigh,
And all the world was given in one warm kiss?*
— *The Light of Asia.*

Young love is the Lethe of sorrow and sadness,
   She smiles and the hot tears forget their quick flow;
Deep wounds are oft healed by the sunshine of gladness,
   Then shun not this balm from a bosom of snow.

The knights of Old Spain sought the Fountain of Youth,
   In lands far from home where summer unending,
Blushed ever with flowers whose perfume, in sooth,
   Was as sweet as the dew on the jasmine sleeping.

But in vain was the search, and they perished at last;
   The secret they knew not, for youth does not flow

From the founts of a land where by chance we are cast,
  Though it sparkle and cheer like old wine in its glow.

In the bowers of Hispania her maids are awake,
  The orange trees breathe their soft perfume around;
Light guitar and castinet harmony make,
  And the gay dance is tripped to voluptuous sound.

The rich wine flows free, but the lips that it stains
  Shame its red hue in depth, in warmth and in glow;
What more could ye want, when worn with war's pains,
  Than to rest by these fountains and all care forego?

Ah, here are the fountains of youth that ye lost,
  In your own sunny land; not in forest and wild,
Where man hath not trod, yet bitter the cost
  To pine with that thirst but forever exiled!

Not in everglades bright with rare flowers, is found
  The draught that shall youth's immortality give;
Go seek it where love and light pleasure abound,
  And innumerate years in one hour you will live.

It dwells in the roses on beauty's soft cheek,
  In the sigh from the bosom, and flash from the eye;
Repose here, O, tired ones, no farther need seek,
  These fountains flow ever, and ever are nigh.

'NEATH THE WILLOWS.

A SUMMER IDYL.

I.

'Neath the willows by the river,
  Where the shadows darkly lie,
Where the dark and gloomy shadows
      Never die;
Where the sunlight's sheen and quiver
Always enters an intruder—
      With a sigh;
There the red-wings pipe in summer,
  Swinging lightly to their cadence,
Far above the drowsy water's
      Faintest accents;
There the naiad's fairest daughters
Lave and sport with strangest laughter's
      Soft allurements.

II.

Meadows sweet with purple clover
  Sloping to the water's edge,
Downward to the scented thyme
      And graceful sedge;
Always beck'ning to the rover,
Sighing to the plaintive plover
      In the hedge;
Come and lounge beneath the willows,
  I will sing while you shall stay;
Toil not in the burning sunshine
      Of the day;
Here are cool, refreshing shadows,
Here are purple, perfumed meadows,
      Come and stay—
      Come and stray,
Where the star-eyed daisies smile,
Where the cat-bird calls the while—
      'Neath the willows.

III.

Drifts a boat a-down the river,
  Underneath the hanging willows,
Light oars break the shimmering surface
      Into billows;
Soft and undulating ever,
In the falling twilight, never
      Sweeter song rose;
Song with two low voices blended,
  One with dreamy echoing flute-notes,
Th' other deep and grand and solemn
      Upward floats; .
But in harmony they ended,
Separate, yet together blended
      From their throats.

IV.

Words like these were borne to me
'Neath the shadows listlessly:
  Come, when the daylight dies,
    Under the star-lit skies,

This is love's own hour,
Who could resist its power?
Not I, not I, while youth shall last;
While passion burns no joy is past.
With silvered locks and age,
Pleasures, no more engage;
Let us love while we live,
What more can earth give?
Then come 'neath the stars on the river's tide,
We'll gather the lotus and sing as we glide;
And, O, the wild rapture—my darling, my bride—
To clasp thee again,
To clasp thee and love thee forever my own,
While life shall remain—
While life with its rosiest chain
Weaves our hearts into one on Hymen's soft throne.

V.

Dies the song's last words in the distance—
Fades their forms in gray and twilight;
Thus their lives drift on together
Glad and bright;

Caught in fancy's web of chance
On this river of romance,
    Free from night;
And each holds the other's heart
Captive as its dearest part.

VI.

Truth to me all this had seemed,
'Neath the willows I'd but dreamed,
    Lounging there this summer reverie,
Pictured pleasures I ne'er deemed
    Could for mortal ever be—
Songs and scenes too sweet to last—
Dreaming, thought I held them fast,
Waking, found them ever past,
    ' And I alone 'neath the willows.

DRIFTING.

We are drifting, love, apart,
   As the ebbing waters flow
Backward from my lonely heart,
   Leaving all my thoughts aglow
With the sands of recollection;
   And the shores are desolate
Where the tide of hope begun,
   Broken now by storms of fate.

O, could I but span the years
   Gone since first as friends we met,
With such bridge as mem'ry rears
   O'er some chasm of regret,
When I feel the sad conviction

Piercing like a poisoned dart,
And I hear the murmured diction—
We are drifting, love, apart.

Drifting, drifting, surely, swiftly,
   From the shores where love has dwelt,
Happy, free and thoughtlessly,
   On that sea the mind has felt
Sweep in surges o'er the past,
   'Till its brighest memories
All are carried with the last,
   Into depths the soul ne'er flees.

Lingers there not, love, one moment
   That the heart can still hold dear,
Neither tainted by lament
   Nor the blight of doubting fear—
That amid a world of care,
   Like a flame in deep recess,
Lights for awhile with dying glare
   Darkness it would fain depress?

Yes, above all life's allurements
    Shines the light of other days,
Flashing brightly through the rents
    Caused by thought where e'er it strays;
Yet there comes when hope looms darkly
    O'er a world where joys depart,
Echoes from the past so dreary—
    We are drifting, love, apart.

A PORTRAIT.

Oft as I look upon this face,
   A thousand joys my mind recalls;
Sweet, happy moments that embrace
   Years in their singleness—enthralls
My feelings with love's lightest chain,
Which tightly binds with willing pain.

Here I can view that sweetest smile
   Which ever won the hearts of all,
And often helps mine to beguile
   Its sadness when a sigh would fall—
That flash of sunshine which dispells
The ebon clouds where doubt oft dwells.

The soft gold falling round her brow,
   In wavy ringlets unconfined,
Marks but one charm youth's beauty now—

In all its lovliness resigned—
Would add to innocence and grace,
Twin virtues of that fairest face.

That form to me, soft Aphrodite,
   With her magic girdle bound,
Rising from out the Grecian sea
   Had circled her slight zone around,
And that enticing power had given
Which now to her my heart has driven.

Yes, e'en though years had passed away
   And this fond gift had ne'er been mine,
Ah, well could I recall the day
   When love and life dwelt e'er with thine,
For now thy form more fair than art,
Shall live forever in my heart.

LONGING.

I am sad to-night, my darling,
    Weary, and my soul rests not,
For thy form haunts all my dreaming,
    Visions throng me unforgot.

Eyes with tender passion beaming,
    Half betray the minds desire,
True and constant without seeming,
    On thy shrine Love lights his fire.

Dark misgivings crowd the mem'ry,
    Hopes and fears each in their turn
War for the ascendency,—
    Still my heart for thee must yearn.

What though cruel disappointment
    Crown at last each dream of bliss,
Shall a thought of harsh resentment
    Give thy lips a Judas kiss?

POEMS OF LOVE.

No, the world, though stern, unfeeling,
    Weaves the lie in truth's fair guise,
I shall ne'er by double-dealing
    Hope to win the humblest prize.

Should the vilest tongue malign thee,
    Spurn it with a high disdain,
Truth shall triumph and assign thee
    All that worth and virtue gain.

Youth denied its spring-time pleasures,
    Love forbidden cannot die;
These, the world's supremest treasures,
    Will surmount adversity.

Let us fill the foaming goblet,
    Drink to all the dear, dead days,
And we'll pledge to ne'er forget
    Joys that brightened all our ways.

Friendship clasped the hand of Fancy,
    Gave no thought for future years;
Heedless though that grasp should bind me,
    Will it end in smiles or tears?

LONGING.

Though to-night I'm sitting lonely,
    Dreaming of the happy past,
Phantoms of the future show me
    All the joys that wait at last.

"Love is enough," my heart is saying,
    Why rebel against decree?
Life can own no truer swaying,
    And my soul still yearns for thee.

Then my heart forget your sighing,
    Love will ever seek its own,
And the years though dark and trying
    Will for all their ills atone.

A GREETING FROM THE SOUTH.

When e'er I think of thee, my love,
    As evening woos the summer sky,
In vain my burning heart can prove
    Its yearnings save with lonely sigh.
O, say, shall I tell thee the day will soon come
When I'll meet thee again in thy own loved home,
And clasp thee again to my bosom so true?
But, O, for tonight, love, adieu, adieu!

The river flowing t'ward the sea
    Forgets too soon its mountain home,
But as I farther stray from thee,
    My thoughts, my dreams to thee still come.
O, could I but see thy dear form once more,
And feel the soft light of the eyes I adore;
O, what could e'er drive me again far and wide
When to live in thy love is worth all life beside.

A GREETING FROM THE SOUTH.

Let hope's balmy touch brush the cares from thy
    brow,
  Like a lover's caress when the soft curls stray,
And I'll love thee as fondly as though I were now
    By thy side, darling Vera, forever to stay.
Yes, yes, I will come ere the roses shall fade,
And if still not to claim thee, the vows that were
    made
I'll renew with devotion, and all that the heart
Can give to its idol, when long drawn apart.

BIRDS OF NIGHT.

I.

O, dreary birds of night,
   Mid storms on gloomy wing,
Whither your lonely flight?
   What thoughts your wild cries bring!

From frozen rivers drear,
   To summer climes you go,
Where Winter comes not near
   And wild-flowers ever blow.

My thoughts are borne with thee
   Mid clouds of darkness and doubt;
To that land of sunshine they flee,
   They dwell on the storms without.

How you, O, birds, recall,
   Sad recollections, sweet,
As you battle the storms that enthrall
   And hope never wanes with defeat.

II.

Years, long years ago, when shone
    Gay youth, a tiny figure stole
Silent, radiant, all unknown,
    And claimed a place within my soul.

She was so young, so pure and fair,
    So shyly beautiful and bright,
That one harsh breath could turn the rare
    Soft sunshine of her life to night.

And yet she knew it not through years,
    Knew not her love like thistle-down,
Borne on the whisp'ring, morning zephyrs,
    Had lodged within my heart, nor flown.

The little wanderer had found
    A home, a resting place secure,
Where love and hope in one were bound,
    Nor separation could endure.

Yes, ever there she has remained,
  Like dew that cheers the drooping flower,
And has for life a lustre gained
  Unknown without affection's bower.

III.

What though the wild-birds scream to-night,
  Their harsh and weird notes of woe ;
What though within a pensive plight
  My mind is carried as they go ?

'Tis only this, that they recall,
  A love that's stronger than my life,
And their strange cries seem like a pall
  That heralds death of hope, and strife.

And yet I know there is no trust,
  No love more pure and true than hers—
My Edith's—though the years still thrust
  Me from her smile, and bring their fears.

BIRDS OF NIGHT.

No more I hear the wail of winds,
   The cries of wild-birds hurrying on ;
Lost in love's reverie nothing binds
   The spirit that would clasp its own.

And still the big drops ceasless beat
   Against the casement, and the trees
Moan piteously amid the sleet
   That falls from black and boreal skies.

FADED ROSES.

SONG.

The roses are sweet though they're faded,
    I would not fling them away,
In my love's fair hair they were braided,
    She gave them at parting today.

With their pale leaves I weave with quick fancy
    The rapture one moment could give,
When the waltz-music sounded so dreamy,
    And life seemed all rythm and love.

Then her head rested close to my shoulder,
    With its gold-waves and roses entwined,
O, the madness their odor breathed ever,
    Like poppies distilled o'er my mind.

And I press to my lips the droop'd petals,
　　And think of the pleasures now past,
When the nights all seemed bright madrigals,
　　Nor doubted such joy could not last.

Shall summer when winter has fallen,
　　Never gladden the days that are dark?
Shall the days that are happy and golden
　　Ne'er illumine the days of dull work?

Who would dash down the wine-cup impatient,
　　And shatter the crystal unfilled?
Has the draught not been drunk with enjoyment,
　　While eyes glanced and bosoms were thrilled?

The waltz will out live its last cadence,
　　Though the ball-room's deserted and still,
And the pressure, the beauty, the movements,
　　Long recur our soft reveries to fill.

Never slight the perfume of dead roses,
　　Nor the fragrance of wine that has glowed,
The sweetest of earth e'er reposes
　　In memory's fancied abode.

Sonnets.

TO ATHENA.

.   .   .   what is writ, is writ,
Would it were worthier.
—*Byron.*

I.

HOPE.

As when misfortune groping in despair,
   Touches the hand of hope, and once again
   Feels sure and safe in all it could attain,
   So you, sweet friend, have led me upward, where
All seemed chaos, every path a snare,
   And bid me trust again, and woke a strain
   Long silent in my heart, free from all pain,
   Till the lax strings again to strike I dare.
Deep feeling courts not words, nor gratitude
   Expression; yet, perchance, thine eyes can read
   More than is writ, and see a striving here,
For that which is not reached, or feebly sued;
   If aught is best, think that the flame was fed
   From thy pure shrine, I claim no portion, dear.

II.

HELLAS.

I see upon the towering, marbled height
   Of Athens' glory—the Acropolis—
   A form majestic, grand and Jove-like this,
   Amid the temples and the fanes of light,
That gave to Greece her prowess and her might
   In arms and art; victorious Salamis,
   The Phidian wonders, the Arcadian age of bliss,
   That from the world forever took their flight.
I see the rude, barbaric warriors mount
   The sacred hill, their hands no mercy know—
   The priests out driven, the vestals violate,
The city given to plunder's dire account—
   All lost, save fragments that through ages glow
   With light divine, nor time obliterate.

III.

HELLAS.

Delphi is desolate! No more shall sound
   The rythmic oracles that told the fate
   Of men and nations, pride and power and state,
   All humbled in the dust; nor scarce is found
A trace of what shall be to ages round
   Wonder of wonders. The earth can find no mate
   For thy blind, wand'ring bard whose songs so great
   In every tongue, in every heart resound.
Thou art not dead, O, Hellas! Life like thine
   Unto thy race is a rich heritage!
   Sappho still sings; Anacreon's lyre of love,
Tuneless through ages, still echoes chords divine!
   Thy sculptured forms, fill yet a nobler page
   Of that proud history time cannot improve.

IV.

HELLAS.

O, could the shades of thy dead past assume
   Their god-like forms, and attributes of power
   That rescued beauty from her lustful dower;
   To Priam's city placed the torch of doom—
And flame and war filled foes with hopeless gloom—
   Greece would be free in that same day and hour!
   Eros, alone, smiles in his sunny bower,
   And blights the manhood that he should illume;
Grim Mars is dead; Apollo is no more;
   The Wingless Victories that crowned the Capitol—
   The trophies thy immortal valor won—
Have crept abject, not flown from off thy shore;
   All these have gone, and naught remains or shall,
   While foreign yoke rests on this land of sun.

V.

APHRODITE.

Not by ignoble worship at the Cyprean shrine,
   Nor fawning at the feet of beauty's queen—
   Though never lured she with such tempting mien—
   Can true ambition ever hope to shine
Upon the tablets of the Sacred Nine:
   Stern sisters they, with face and brow serene,
   Who own no half devotion ; it must wean
   The world and the soft breast where pleasures twine
Their rosiest garlands with seductive smile,
   Till youth forgets—though dreams he sweetest there,
   And fancy builds in clouds its lofty towers—
Lost is the power to act ; manhood the while
   Forsakes him, and the visioned fame so fair,
   Bursts like a bubble mid these wanton hours.

VI.

VIRGINIA.

Land of my birth! with trembling hand I twine
   These homely wreaths to place upon thy brow!
   Ah, small the honor I could bring thee now—
   Thy errant son—by aught that I enshrine,
Though all the power of every age combine
   To pour through this my verse's sluggish flow;
   The past has filled thy annals with a glow
   Time shall not dim though all should rival thine!
O, from this deep, lethargic slumber rise!
   Shake off the shackles that would drag thee down!
   They futnre yet shall glorious be and proud
Even as thy past! Ope but the closèd eyes!
   Lo, Nature gives thee all; no part has flown!
   Put regal garments on, cast off thy shroud!

VII.

VIRGINIA.

The blow that broke the Afric's galling chain,
   And raised him from the serfdom where he wrought,
   Has not loosed thine, the slavery of thought;
   Its swift wheels never can be stayed again
While progress holds the lash; why not be taught?
   Why still refuse the lesson thy blood bought?
   Dwell not upon the past, such act were vain;
   What can it bring thee now, what e'er attain?
Forget thy pride! It only can degrade,
   Unless it serve as impetus to deeds
   That emulate the great of other days.
The present calls thee, all thy latent aid
   The nation waits to add to her great needs,
   And haste the glory that thy sloth delays.

VIII.

MONTECELLO.

I stand on hallowed ground; there is not here,
   Within this wide domain historic, found,
   A spot more sacred to the pilgrim bound
   For liberty's most reverenced shrine and dear—
Save one, Mount Vernon, resting ever near
   The blue Potomac. Dense the hill is crowned
   With the venerable oaks that shade the mound
   Where sleeps the friend of man who knew no fear.
The soft June morn rests on the peaceful valley;
   It is a glorious prospect! Far away
   The purple mountains and the welkin blend;
Earth may have fairer scenes—though few they be—
   But the proud world can boast no son to-day
   More worthy of its homage or his end.

IX.

CHIPPEWA.

Sitting alone within the shady wood
   I watched the sun go down beyond the lake—
   A scene of such sweet calmness it could wake
   Melody from hushed lips—and such a mood
Stole o'er me there, gazing upon the flood
   Of roseate, golden light that seemed to break
   Upon the water, that no art could make
   More lovely in its every change that woo'd.
The trees upon the distant, fading shore,
   And sloping meadows glowing with their wealth
   Of purple clover still uncut, were all
Reflected in the changeless face it bore;
   The twilight fell, and with redoubled stealth
   The shadows crept from out the nightly pall.

X.

CHIPPEWA.

Ling'ring, I watched the moon's pale crescent rise,
   Shrouded in amber mist, above the trees;
   I could have wished them ever, moments like these,
   When the tired heart reads in the starry eyes
That gaze upon him, hints of the infinities,
   And then will mount superior to decrees
   Of flesh, and earth's desponding tendencies—
   Accepting all, nor humblest will despise.
The lights began to glimmer through the grove,
   And then, from the pavillion, softly rose
   Orchestral music; fainter I could hear
At intervals, the sounds of feet that love
   Harmonious movements, and delight that knows
   No joy more sweet, no pleasure half so dear.

XI.

CHIPPEWA.

Musing, I heeded not the hours flew fast,
   Nor cared; it seemed all one could hope or wish;
   And yet, sometimes, soft o'er the soothing hush
   Of this sweet reverie, there would steal at last,
A longing vague, that whispered of a past,
   Completer happiness, with luring sound,
   'Till I forgot the beauty spread around,
   And all but this, the lonely, sad contrast.
But hush! See, through the woody vista trips
   A white-rob'd figure, yet with feet so light
   That scarce a leaf stirred along her way;
A hand steals into mine; warm lips meet lips—
   A thrill—a joy!—Lost was the beauteous night,
   The stars faded, music vain discordancy.

XII.

SALUTATION.

To you who with unfeignèd friendship strove,
    And kind endeavor, my lone life to cheer
    When home was distant with its memories dear,
    And every pleasure truest freedom gave,
Where mountains vied in blue the ocean's wave,
    And the Potomac, calm and crystal clear
    Flowed 'neath high piny cliffs where eagles rear
    Their fearless young, and I as free to roam.
I miss the mountains now, I miss the love
    Of those with whom my earliest years were spent;
    But when I find staunch friends, as I have found,
Where lewd suspicion makes of truth a slave,
    And slander's tongue to every ear is bent,
    I gain new courage for the day's dull round.

XIII.

CONSTANCY.

Can we be false to one another, Love,
    When all the world seems soulless, and of stone
    The hearts where tenderness should live alone;
    And in their petty strife the good dissolve
That should ennoble, not degrading prove?
    How small the compass that confines the tone
    Of their pent lives—the natures that disown
    All human harmony—discordant grown
By their own hate and venomed jealousy,
    Fling open wide the Janus-gates of strife,
    And pitying Peace forever driven away!
No, Love must bind with truest constancy,
    The wounds that silent grieve away the life,
    And thus defeat will mock the spoiler's play.

XIV.

A TRIBUTE.

What shall I give to thee whose form, whose soul,
   Whose beauty soft as twilight dreams of love
   Filled with the beings of some sphere above,
   Impells each aspiration t'ward its goal;
Restrains me when the fiercer passions roll
   Within my breast, and every good can prove—
   Ambition, hope—all that for which I strove
   To raise my life and form a perfect whole?
For thee I tune my long neglected lute,
   But strive in vain to sing becoming praise;
   And O, how poor such homely chords must seem,
For thy charms make the strings forever mute,
   And dull, and soulless; and these simple lays
   Are but the echo of that twilight dream.

XV.

YOU BID ME SING.

You bid me sing: can broken heart-strings thrill
  With rhymèd words and soft, caressing songs—
  Low murmured love—which to the god belongs
  Whose blinded sight can see no eyelids fill
With sad, salt tears and spirit-breaking ill—
  When every pulse-throb but recalls my wrongs,
  My withered hopes, the joyless nights day brings,
  And drives all harmony far from my will?
Ah, Love, there was a heavenly time to me,
  When first I saw thy beauty in my dreams,
  That shed a radiance o'er my darkest days;
Then I beheld strange melodies in thee,—
  Faintest, intangible, unearth-born forms—
  Songs that no mortal pens for human lays.

XVI.

THE PAST.

Come to me, Love, and let me kiss away
    The cares that rob me of the smile that erst
    Did greet me, long—so long ago—when first
    At eve we walked beneath the silvered ray
Of stars mysterious; and for the day,
    No thought would take, if love's unsated thirst,
    But for an hour were slaked in streams that burst
    From deep, full hearts, where feeling has its sway.
I look upon the past—which is not past,
    Or ne'er can be while memory still is true
    To its glad days, and peace which comes no more—
With longing that with every change must last,
    And dwarf the pleasures that the years shall strew
    Along my path, though brightest hues they wore.

XVII.

BEAUTY.

Beauty, I know not what thou art, nor care;
   Demon or god, alone I worship thee!
   And helpless own they lordly mastery.
   Yet this I know, thou art supremely fair,
Making all pale beside thy radiance rare;
   Teach me thy secrets, I thy slave will be,
   Renouncing all if once thy form I see,
   Yet such a boon no mortal hopes to share.
I saw a face that the Greek gods might own
   With pride, so pure and placid in each line,
   And calm and fair as Psyche; then, again, I turned
And looked; lo, all had fled; even cold as stone
   It seemed, and soulless; yet, I still seek thine,
   Following a fantasy, perchance, though warned.

XVIII.

RESOLUTION.

Life is a troubled sea, and restless, so
   Despair oft comes, and hope lies but a wreck
   Of bitter aspirations, that bedeck
   The shores of desolation and of woe,
Where late the buoyant, laughing flow
   Of spirits ran, and swept away all thought
   That in our lives this darkest color wrought,
   And like a mourning mantle weighs us low.
Is this man's end, to sink? His destiny
   Demands an effort worthy of the name,
   To which posterity can point and say;
Here was a man who fought the hard decree
   Of fate unflinchingly, victorious came
   From each fierce battle, with an added ray.

XIX.

HEBE.

O, sprite of beauty flitting through my dreams—
  Sweet Tantala—I e'er could fondly fold
  In warm embrace thy fairy, wanton mould!
  To kiss thy taunting lips so tempting seems,
That I would brave the sacred, sylvan streams
  Where Dian laves—tho' who so brave,
  Upon her naked loveliness untold,
  Once gazing, loses life's dear flame.
So, Actaeon-like, would I surrender all
  If to thy bower my footsteps I could speed,
  And drink deep draughts of love from thy sweet lips
Where none could hear our sighings softly fall—
  Mingling with fragrance from the flowery mead—
  While joy from every fount new pleasure sips.

XX.

HEBE.

The liquid languor of thine eyes, infinite
   In change, and playful, deep as azure ocean;
   Soft as the hyacinthine-perfumed lotion
   That steals our senses in a may-time night;
Or like the violet's more modest fright
   Hiding amid the grass in shyest notion—
   So art thine eyes to me with every motion,
   Shedding or shutting out their subtle light.
Thrilled as I gaze, no mortal power could bind
   Me like their siren, silent playfulness.
   That seems to draw and hold me like twin stars
At which we look till dazzled and quite blind,
   Striving like old astrologers to guess
   What horoscope awaits our sinking fears.

XXI.

NO LOVE IS LOST.

No love is lost though it sleep on forever
   In some shut breast, sighing the while it sleeps,
   Yearning for joys some other always reaps;
   Fleeing like fragrance the touch to the sense would deliver;
And inarticulate, complaining never,
   In endless dream Endymion-like, that steeps
   Existence all in bliss, but never leaps
   Within the wave of passion's restless river.
Though saddest heart should weep my years away
   And broken vows be all that's left to me,
   I know my love will live and love again
When nature shall dissolve in voiceless clay,
   And be a portion of infinity,
   Undying but beyond all mortal ken.

XXII.

LOVE IMMORTAL.

I know my love shall never fade and die
    And sink like flowers that blush but for a day,
    Lost to all sense, forever past away
    Nor having aught of color or of beauty—
Ephemeral things, true-called of human frailty
    The emblem. This I feel and always say;
    My love immortal is, and so shall play
    A part in lives unborn, unknown to me.
O, sweet consoling thought! That though my love
    No echo finds in a harsh world of doubt,
    And never feels the sympathy it yearns,
That, Phœnix-like, I know 'twill rise above
    Decay of matter, and chains doubly stout,
    And clasp the form for which it ceasless burns.

XXIII.

EMERSON.

Behold, even in this scandalous, Sceptico-Epicurean generation, where all is gone but hunger and cant, it is still possible that Man be a man.—Carlyle.

He was a man; and of that high and noble state,
   That pure simplicity, seeming most near
   Divinity—an essence of his clear
   Unfeigned philosophy—and in each trait
Nearing the true ideal that must await
   The ages still unborn, ere it uprear
   Its image as a guide to those who hear,
   But feebly understand his mission great.
Nor since those days when in the Attic groves,
   Or by the cooling streams, resting at noon,
   The old philosophers of Hellas sought
For truth untrammeled, none but he has thrown
   Such light along this path where seldom roves
   The bravest foot, for else to him was naught.

XXIV.

MOIRAE.

O, Clotho, backward turn thy rapid wheel
   Which bears me on through time ignobly spent!
   The golden sands by hand infinite lent,
   Have darkened by a touch unknown to weal,
Or aught of joy that life of fame can feel.
   A tide of woe now covers all, and rent,
   The spirit, with its weight of conscience bent
   Bows' low, this burning chastisement to feel.
And thou Atropos, with the scale of time
   Still held aloft in wavering fitful hand—
   The fate of mortals and their destiny
To weigh impartially—now in my prime
   Thy doom delay, or yet with grave command
   The brittle thread is broke, the spirit free.

XXV.

YOUTH'S LOVE.

When Love first dwelt in Eden's fragrant bowers,
    Untainted yet by act or thought profane—
    Free as a bird ere yet by hunter slain,
    Mounting to heights beyond recurrent showers—
Where innocence beguiled the happy hours
    With sweetest trust, no care, but to remain
    In confidence secure, the world's disdain,
    I knew the bliss where time nor fame e'er towers.
To thee I turn like one who's wandered long
    In distant lands and many a pleasure known,
    And drank the fragrance of enticing rounds
Till joy had weary grown with its own throng
    Of happiness; remorseful and alone,
    I haste return to feel thy soothing bonds.

XXVI.

THE FLIGHT OF YEARS.

O, how this troubled wave of changeful years,
    Swift bear us on its gloomy, moaning breast,
    From childhood on to manhood, without rest
    And ofttimes hope; and dark, perplexing fears
Guard every step as our too willing ears
    Heed faintest callings with our youthful zest,
    Till sparkling pleasure is the goddess blest,
    And deep remorse ends life, and penal tears.
Shall it be so? or shall the nobler man
    Assert its high supremacy, and urge
    Ambition to a loftier, truer plane,
Where honor, fame and love, greet that proud van
    Triumphant, and the black'ning, damning surge
    Rolls back, and manhood claims its sway again?

XXVII.

EPIGRAM.

I heard a hard and cruel man once say—
   One who had spent his life in gain of gold,
   While with one hand he of his wealth untold,
   Seemed lavish to the poor, the other's play
Upon the widow's meagre purse hard lay.
   Secure in luxury and scheming bold,
   Gave not a thought of how her deep tears rolled,
   And wrung from her the pittance saved away;—
I heard this man say to the youths around,
   Be just, and to the needy freely give,
   And it shall be tenfold returned to you;
Which meant: to Mammon's shrine be firmly bound,
   Heed not the heart, and you shall surely live
   Honored by all, despised by self—your due.

XXVIII.

APOLLO SCORNED.

Fair girl, why now Apollo, joyful, shun,
   Or slight the muse whom Bacchus loves to crown?
   When mirth and joy with gayety can drown
   All sadness though by gloomy care begun;
Who thrilled Terpsichore, the maid that won
   The hearts of many an age with flowing gown
   And grace inimitable, as adown
   The avenues of pleasure gaily run.
To him, then, turn thy accents, soothing, mild,
   There linger with him in his shady bowers;
   Delight awakened with his harp will fill
Thy breast with transport, feeling doubly wild,
   And often help thee to beguile the hours
   When loneliness seeks to depress the will.

Sylvan.

ELYWOOD.

This is the regal season of the four;
The air is laden with the breath of flowers,
And myriad bees hum round the honey'd cells
Of thistle and of clover.   Noiseless still,
Flitting from bloom to bloom, the butterfly
Feeds on the dainty sweets, but hoards no store
Against the coming storms of winter months—
Bright, thoughtless things, that glad the gazing eye
A moment, and are gone.

                     Beneath the pines,
I lie and muse and watch the scene outspread
Alternately; each hath its subtle charm.
Now, while I look, my errant fancy strays
Far from the wood and placid stream close by;
And oft in strange rebellion would assume
Control of sight that leads it back to earth,
For here is beauty it were mockery

For man to shun.   Nature has been lavish;
From the high cliffs where cling the grappling pines,
Down to the mirror'd rocks and swaying reeds,
All must delight and satisfy the soul
Of him who worships in these sylvan shrines.
Beyond the river stretch the verdant meads,
Whereon the kine are grazing; silence sways
A tyrant sceptre, for no sound is heard,
Save when a plaintive low at intervals
Comes from the meadows, yet no discord this,
But seems a tone in nature's harmony.

To me these are familiar haunts and loved;
Their every path is known, each shady glen,
Where sunshine dares not come; the warmest slopes,
Where bloom the earliest flowers, ere winter's snows
Have scarcely gone, and first the violets
Ope their blue eyes to feel the light again,
And the anemones star all the sward,
Till Autumn paints her fleeting colors here,
And leaves the knarled trunks naked to the wind.
Each tree, each gray and moss-grown rock; the vines
That droop in graceful festoons from the boughs—

Whereon bright Ariel might swing and watch
The silvery moon—the thickets by the stream,
Where bends the light witch-hazel o'er the bank;
Each feathery fern and spray of golden-rod,
That summer strews so lavish, seem as friends,
And in their silence speak with words as clear
As ever fell from tongue of eloquence;
But, most of all, upon yon towering hill,
Pine-covered and rock-riven, I could look
And dream away a life. What tales the winds—
Ceaselessly sighing through their deep, dark, shades—
They tell, as year by year goes round, and still,
Changeless amid change, they ever stand!

Oft have I started from some reverie broke
By laughter ringing through the quiet woods,
And strained my eyes to catch the sight of nymphs
Sporting in these retreats, as the old legends tell
Of fair Arcadian groves; but naught could see
More than some thoughtless children by the stream,
Unawed by their own echoes; for no more
The wood-gods haunt the forest as in days
When life was still untrammeled by the laws

Which strive to fashion all by one set mould,
And leave no nature in the man.   In vain
Ye look for shaggy Pan and his gay train
Of jolly bacchanals; no more you hear
His reedy syrinx, flute-like, echoing now,
And see the wild dance in the shady glades;
And fawn and satyr all have disappeared.
Those days are past—the golden, glorious days
Of legend and of myth.   Yet he who loves
The forests and the streams with true devotion
Longs for this age again, which ne'er will come,
With all its beings of the border world,
That lived in fountains and in gloomy caves,
And peopled every grove with forms poetic.

Ye marvel at the art this age produced,
Its marble temples and its palaces;
Its statues, God-like in their majesty,
And all the fragments that the centuries
Have spared from countless devastating wars
And their barbaric pillage; yet the page
Of history is plain.   They sought not wealth,
But beauty; striving to realize in form

The pure ideal of exalted mind,
Unbiased, warped not by a culture false,
And that penurious grasping after gold
Which fawns to folly and crude patronage.
Not art alone, but perished with it here,
The grand old epics of heroic song,
Not less in simple dignity and power.
And they who sought for truth renouncing life,
To gain such feeble light as slowly comes
From meditation and self-abnegation—
Buddh, Socrates, his true disciple, Plato,
Zeno and Aristotle; scarce less than these,
In later age, Mahomet—all are names
The world must reverence till the end of time.

Long centuries must lapse ere spirits bold
And high as these shall rise, and once again,
Reclaim the world from its desponding way.
When avarice is surfeited, and wealth
Is weary of its gaudy ostentation—
Vainest of all delusions—and luxury
Has shaken off effeminating robes, ·
And the tired earth shall pause for rest again,

And mind take up the sceptre swayed by gold,
Teaching mankind to follow Nature's ways
And seek its truths; renouncing a false life
As it would spurn a false god from its faith.
Till such a state the future nations claim,
Nor art nor deep philosophy can reign.

But I have wandered; and the trackless ways
Where meditation strays through the dim past,
Now hazy with its many centuries,
Dealing with forms long perished from our life,
Are not so clear to me as the cool woods,
Where every path is known.

        Here, oft alone,
I come when the harsh, grating world would weigh
Too heavy on the heart, and bruise the springs
Of feeling. Lying here, I can forget
All save the beauty of the scene below—
Its soothing stillness and the peaceful hours—

And yet, the city with its busy throng,
Is scarce a bow-shot from this shady bank,
And through the vista of the winding stream
The gray church-spire is outlined on the sky.

JULY, 1885.

GATHERING ARBUTUS.

I.

O, what can equal a bright day in Spring,
   A drive to the mountains when Winter has fled
Like a white-whinged phanton, or echoes that ring
    Through the groom of the forest and fill us with dread;
When Nature comes forth from her drear hiding place,
Free and smiling once more from a snowy embrace;

When the streamlets that play in the rugged ravines,
   Leap with unfettered grace to the valleys below,
As with innocent wonder inquiring the means
    That had loosed them, ice-bound, and made them to flow
With merrier song from their high rocky home,
Like children set free in wild-wood to roam.

GATHERING ARBUTUS.

When the mist gathers soft o'er the far distant hills,
   Till they blend with the sky in obscurity dim—
And with dreamiest beauty the whole landscape fills;
   When the wind murmurs soft through the pines dark and grim,
Then seek silent nature, her lone, shady haunts,
Where wild flowers grow nor vain fashion flaunts.

II.

When fair Aurora scarce yet had oped
   The roseate gates of dewy morn,
And Phoebus shining from the East had hoped
   To gladden earth with day new born,
All where prepared to leave the city's bounds
To revel in sweet nature's rounds:

Such bright young faces beaming with delight,
   Eyes sparkling in their very happiness;
Warm, glowing heart's love ne'er could slight
   If tempted far by their own loveliness—
For they, too, wore the spring-time beauty,
And youth had crowned them with his gayety.

We now had reached the rugged woodland,
    Had reached the mountains wild and budding
To life their branches rough and grand,
    And trunks that through long centuries standing,
Storms born from northern seas had braved,
And winds that through their boughs fierce raved.

We paused by the spring from the hill-side flowing,
    On the green mossy bank we there sat down,
Where nature, solemn, silent, throwing
    O'er all her sadness, seemed to drown
All merriment within her stillness,
And our light hearts in thought depress.

III.

The hawthorn buds just opening lay,
    Like snowflakes on the half bare limbs,—
Which spring, forgetful of the day
    Had left alone, nor beauty dims—
And golden-rods were waving by the streams
Bright sceptres of the nymphic realms.

GATHERING ARBUTUS.

The dreamy dogwood blossoms spread
   Their pale, soft petals in the light,
And where the path by the water led,
   The lilies there, yet hid from sight,
Were sending up their leaves to be
Borne on the waves so gracefully.

But fairer still than these, by far,
   Half hid beneath its leaves of green—
Where mossy rocks its charms would bar—
   The sweet Arbutus flower is seen;
So modest, yet so beautiful it lay
Down close to earth in clustering spray.

I almost shrank from robbery
   Which seemed so cruel and unkind,
When it was striving willingly
   Earth to adorn with life refined—
The wild and barren heath to dress
In simple, graceful loveliness.

I, bending down, would pluck the flower
    From many a crevice out of sight,
While Vera, standing near, the dower
    Within her dainty hand clasped tight,
Burst forth in admiration wild,
And tighter pressed the captive mild.

And as she thanked me in delight,
    Her rapture caring not to hide,
Or blush that came in rosy might
    Upon her fair young cheek, or tide
Of pleasure flowing fond and free,
All whispering love so innocently.

Not far below us in the marsh,
    Jack-in-the-pulpit sternly stood,
And loud he preached in numbers harsh
    To dreamy list'ners of the wood;
The oak-tree nodded its assent,
While hemlock wondered what he meant.

And such a man in such a dress!
   I know not yet his theme or text,
Nor what great truth sought to express;
   How long he talked or what came next,
All were unheard, for what cared we
Both bound in love so happily.

The sun sank low behind the ridge;
   The shadows lengthen'd o'er the plain;
And far away a golden bridge
   Seemed linking hill and mount again,
While all below lay shadowy
And lost to color's varied play.

We wander'd back, the party gained,
   And homeward then again we started,
While merriment through forest reigned
   And Flora from her haunts was frighted;
The gloomy pine-trees sighed—farewell!
And dreamy woods their echos swell.

Gettysburgh, Pa., 1879.

THE ADVENT OF SUMMER.

From tropic climes resplendent with the sun,
   Thy gilded, glittering car rolls swiftly on :—
The herald of bright days and season born
   For southward, where forever cease to dawn
Sweet nature's verdant forms and brightest hues ;—
   And like an odor breathed from Indian isles,
Rich with the balmy breath of spicy dews,
   Thou comest to us, O, season of fair hopes.

THE POET'S PATH.

The silent woods whose shadows now invite
My straying steps from highway's dust and light,
Can teach me more than peopled city's hosts,
Or all the learning that a century boasts.

The trees, the rocks, the grass, the bursting flowers,
And e'en the solitudes, the gloomy bowers
Of interlacing boughs and clambering vines,
Speak each their language if the soul inclines.

The lofty mind is most alone when in
The whirl of multitudes, the ceaseless din
Of jostling commerce and the bustling mart,
Where contemplation has but ill a part.

But wind and wood and undulating plain—
The star-illumined vault, the battling main
That beats with fury on a rocky shore—
Are sympathies, like friends long loved of yore.

But hard the fate, gloomy the hostile path
That he must lead, and brave the ignorant wrath
Of ingrate foes whose souls are naught but clay,
And stupid, beast-like, stand and hoarsely bray.

Envy, her dread companion, sullen Hate,
By his advancing footsteps lie in wait,
To hurl foul calumny upon his deeds,
Nor caring aught how deep his nature bleeds.

Then what is homage, what is earthly fame
That man should strive to win himself a name?
And woo the muse to aid his heavenward flight,
And build his name above oblivious night?

O, better far, the days of peaceful love,
Than toil and struggles that will joyless prove,
And fill youth with unrest and aging care
When life should know naught but the pure and fair.

NATURE'S FREEDOM.

Who ever drank from crystal founts that gush
From mountains wild, where calm and hush
Spread over all the spirit of their rest,
And thirsts for stagnant draughts with former zest?

Who in the freedom of his humble state
Longs for the splendor of the gilded great?
And pines away in sighing for the place
That epmty fashion fills but to disgrace?

Who ever felt the fire of burning love
Thrill to his touch, and farther cared to prove
The callous hearts that would disdain its ways,
Prefering self, and lone secluded days?

Who on the deep, mysterious wave of song
Hath felt his spirit mount above the throng,
And hurried where the restful shores unfold,
Looks back with longing for the greed of gold?

Ambition has its fire which naught can bind,
And rules the heart with eyes to justice blind,
And sated not with conquest on each shore,
Consumes itself, more wretched than before.

There is no more than this, to be content,
And let the mind be always upward bent;
No matter where the path, each leads to truth,
And gives pure peace when age succeeds to youth.

Then seek no more; not all the fabled joys
That sensuous Cyprus in her rites employs,
Nor Daphnean groves that woo with wanton sight,
Can him estrange who once has felt its might.

MORN.

O, thou resplendent morn!
   Being of light and joy supreme,
   O, how the earth as from a dream,
Greets thee as thou adorn
The hills from darkness born,
   And up the sky thy glories stream!

Each fiery, gleaming light
   That burns in the dark sky, is led
   To rest where night has quickly fled,
And all her gloomy might—
In swift and sure affright—
   Vanishing as thy beams outspread.

How sweet the songs of birds
   That greet the tranquil morn now breaking!
   And roseate nature from her sleep awaking!
The distant low of herds;
The belt that brightly girds
   The East, its joyous way betaking!

The wild fowl startled in the brake,
　　Sends forth its long shrill cry and hastens
　　To North-land where the dim, cool glens
Of sombre pine-trees, take
The deep reflected lake
　　Within their dark impenetrable fens.

The mist along the river
　　Gleams with the light of rising beams,
　　And like an airy flood now seems
To hang above and quiver
All radiant, and ever
　　To wane along the murmuring streams.

The bellowing herds, the hills
　　All sparkling with the dew, eager
　　They climb, as if to greet more near
The rising orb that fills
Forest and vale, then dwells
　　In glory while the worlds revere.

What joy to some lone heart,
   Saddened by grief. or disappointed
   Hopes, thou bringest, though peace has fled,
As brightly, quickly dart
Thy red beams in the Orient apart,
   Illumining their lives so dead !

NATURE HEALETH.

Can the tired heart ever find
Full companionship in mind,
That shall quiet all unrest
With the noblest and the best?
Can the lore of ages stay
Longings for a purer ray,
That shall fill the soul with peace
Give to earthly cares release;
All-sufficient, filling all
Though the direst ills befall?
Vain one, no.   Learn this as truth;
Nature can alone lost youth
Reinstate in care-worn breasts.
Why not heed its kind behests?
Delve down deep or upward soar,
Beauty find unknown before:
Music poets never wrote

Gushes from the songster's throat;
Breaks upon the morning air
Melodies no transcript bear,
And will raise thy burdened heart
Out of grief and sorrow's part.
Walk into the star-lit morn
Ere the sun—the Orient-born—
Scatters all the sparkling dew,
Read its lessons ever new—
Older than the ages primal
And the wheeling orbs coeval.
Every leaf and blade of grass
Strives to whisper as you pass,
Alchemy of life and death—
And their restoration hath
Here embodied every change,
In the elemental range.

None my secrets ever know
Who the world will not forego,
And the hermit in his cave
Will excel the grasping slave.
I will teach you, sayeth she,

If alone you follow me;
No divison I will take,
Full surrender you must make;
Walk with me and clasp my hand,
I will close the magic band,
And intuitive will teach
Wonders that no art can reach;
Unseen lips will whisper thee
Of the spheric mystery,
And the eternal course of things
Tending to concentric rings;
How each swaying pine and oak
Form in part this cosmic yoke;
How the lowliest thing of earth—
Like the proudest hath its birth;
As the change eternal goes
Each from out the other flows—
All dependent, all depend,
One must to the other lend;
And no conflict here is found,
Merging and emergent round.
This I teach to all who come
To the groves and silent roam,

And will add the poet's tongue
That my promptings may be sung.
Woo the world no more for rest,
I will show thee what is best,
And infuse thy soul with love
That no earthly change can move.

LIGHT.

I.

The morning breaks! and lo, from out the gates
   Of purple Orient, the god of day
   Bursts forth in gorgeous, flaming panoply!
His light no sluggish slumberer awaits,
But mounts from lowly wood to highest peak
Dispelling gloom and strengthening the weak.
O'er fields of waving grain and streams and lakes,
Illuming worlds, his kingly way he takes,
And pausing not until his labors done—
His mission ended and his course is run—
Then dying on the ocean's foam-tossed breast
Invites the weary to repose and rest.

II.

The poet speaks! and lo, from out the soul,
   A flood of song bursts forth like minstrelsy,
   And many a burden'd heart's made glad and free.

The passions soften, and the far off goal
Of high endeavor seems within the reach—
And truely, too, if seer's words can teach—
Of lowest destiny and humblest power ;
This to the ages is his princely dower ;
Beauty and light, and hope and consolation—
Nor is stern Truth allowed emancipation—
All nature does him homage for he leads
Mankind to higher life and nobler deeds.

Gross matter cannot feed our very life—
The soul—for lust and hate and deadly strife,
Displace the good within if left alone,
Nor weath, nor fame for this can e'er atone.

Occasional Pieces.

TITUS LIVIUS—A REQUIEM.

Written for the "Cremation Exercises" of the class of '83 at Pennsylvania College, June, 1880.

O, thou of Latuim loved in ages gone!
When time was young, nor yet the radiant dawn
Of centuries was clouded by dark wrong:—
When Sappho had in Greece awoke the song
Which echoed round her thousand isles of lore;
When Aneas, his wand'rings just before,
The great Cis-Alpine bard had sounded far,
And mingled with the din of Eastern war
Which lighted Troy with many a blazing ship,
Till god-like Hector passed from lip to lip,
And Grecian warriors and their deeds sublime
Were heard in every age, in every clime;
And highest honor to their names was owned,
And heros with immortal gods were throned;—

Then thou arose, O, Clio, sacred muse,
And taught the Roman thy exalted use;
Taught him the story of his nation's birth,
Its rise, its progress, battles, wars, and worth,
From that far time when he from Ilian flames
Trough Aegean sea, had fled to Latin realms,
Bearing the household gods remembered still
'Mid war's dire fortune, to the sacred hill;
Till Dursius from Italian power was torn,
And Roman arms beyond the Rhine were borne.

    We kneel, O, muse, before thy altar low,
With hearts bowed down, and spirits that aglow
With joy and youthful vigor follows fast
Through every scene and deeds which are the last;
We own, great Jove, thy most exalted power,
The fate's decree, nor urge thy wrathful hour.
With speed to come.

    In Tempe's lovely vale,
From Ossa to Olympus' height, the wail
Of sorrow rang, for here Apollo lone
Had come; the god in deep dejection thrown

His favorite haunt once more had visited,
For thither had his sorrowing footsteps led.
And now his lyre had tuned ; the chords were wrung,
With quivering hand ; a mournful dirge was sung
For him whom Clio loved and early taught
How to narrate great deeds with valor fraught,
In days when Rome her greatest glory knew,
And Art and War their blended roses strew
O'er fair Italia, 'till the Parian mines
Brought forth their matchless gods in southern climes,
To grace the land, the wonder of the age ;
And Scipio, the victor and the sage
Paraded Rome in grand, triumphal show,
And through the streets pressed eager crowds to know
Of conquests on the Carthagenian shore,
And rose a shout unknown to her before.

    When his last notes were hushed, the echo flown,
And he with nature there was left alone—
Bright Phœbus with his gilded chariot sunk
Beneath the far Atlantic's wave, still drunk

With splendor where the light had lingered still;
His trembling fingers struck a grieving thrill,
And as it fell upon the Penean wave,
The dying murmur found its only grave
Upon the ocean's broad and troubled breast,
Where this sad strain was drifting, slowly, blest
With its escape from such a scene. The tress
Along the bank unmovèd by the breeze,
Bowed down until they touched the water where,
The gathering shades had turned to blackness there,
Its gleaming spray.

     Such was the ancient song
That told the grief of gods, the muse's wrong,
When he who now before us on the pyre
First fled from life and all its fond desire,
To sail upon the gloomy Stygian lake
Till dawn. should with its brightest lustre break
Upon the Islands of the Blessed, clear,
And hail the unknown shore with joy more near.
This was the golden age of Roman power,
That knew no bounds, and to the latest hour
Both song and story give immortal praise:

Then she her grandest triumphs sought to raise
In marble palaces; and yet has towered
The Colliseum with such beauty dowered,
That now the moon-beams all the night watch play
Through rents in this vast ruin, where the gay
Throngs of Rome met to witness scenes inhuman;
When victors by the rites of war's dire plan
Brought home the spoils of battle from the Rhone,
And captives from the Danube, who alone
In the blood-stained arena lions fought
Mid cheers that echoed round her walls, bought
By him, torn from his native land and free,
Thus butchered for Rome's high festivity.
And such it was; so if the pilgrim halt
Within its desolation, deem it no fault
If he be tempted to digress, in praise
And admiration, soaring to heights that raise
Its glory and its shame above the dust
Where its far-reaching arches with the rust
Of time have crumbled.

     Why should we not bear
This offering to the gods, and with the glare

Of torch and flame, light up the nightly sky,
Wafting to regions of infinity
This wanderer of our youth mid classic lore,
Where oft ambitious feet have trod before
Seeking the paths of glory?

                                   One moment
Let my sad theme a various thought augment;
One moment let it turn to those who long,
Have hand in hand the Gallic, grievous wrong,
Together plodded through, and Virgil's lay,
"Arms and the man I sing;" and here to-day
Have triumphed in the grandest fight of all,
And witness now this last and final fall,—
May each endeavor meet reality,
And thy ambitions, hopes of bright futurity,
Life's noblest work engage; and now farewell!
Bright, happy scenes; ah, who can tell
The pangs that long may linger in the heart,
Where first we feel, how soon from all to part.

AMBITION.

Youth yearns for greatness as the bee,
   By winter's storms incarcerate,
Sighs for the spring-time to be free
   And summer blossoms all too late.

Beneath the rustic's homely garb
   The mind oft mounts beyond its sphere,
And toil and care but form a barb
   To urge endeavor from the rear.

Scorn not the poor; they labor best—
   Though humble be their station here,
And pride would grind them in the dust—
   Who serve with patience, deaf to fear.

But they who fire sedition's pile
   With envious hearts and lawless hands—
Disowning right and truth the while,
   Can never rise where honor stands.

THE FALLEN.

"The moths eat the ermine, and the world kisses the leper on both cheeks."

O, lift them up—the helpless ones—
They are not wholly lost but fallen;
And would the hand that always shuns,
Reach to their depth, the life begun
In infamy's revolting way,
Might still be rescued ere the cloud
Of sin o'ershadow all its day,
And death alone and misery's shroud
Be all that's left to save them from the crowd.

In pity stay the scorning tongue!
Know ye the grief they inward bear;
How agony's hot tears have wrung

Their hearts though lost to all that's fair?
Let him first fling the stone whose deeds
Know not reproach, nor from the path
Has strayed where willing pleasure leads;
How great the mercy, small the wrath
Would then encounter those who heedless hath!

Help them to rise to honor's place;
Help them to gain what they have lost.
Perhaps the wretchedness ye trace
Is but the price that passion cost,
That gushed from feeling's deepest fount,
And yielding to its soothing thrill,
Forgot the height it had to mount—
Forgot the sovereign power of will—
In that wild clasp which to release would kill.

Too deeply human! Ah, the fault
So few can share with self and soul
Shut in hard breasts, who never halt
Nor look behind upon the goal

The outcast follow driven down
From deep to deeper infamy ;
And who can blame them if they drown
Their woes, their deep despondency
In suicidal act,—they would be free.

Think you the cold and scheming lives,
That circumspect with godly mien,
Parade in every walk that thrives,
And fawn and flatter when they're seen,
But in the secret, sacred way
Of home and calm domestic joys,
Stab in the dark, the traitor play
To every impulse love alloys,
Each sympathy and feeling strife destroys ;

Think you their lot an envied one ?
Deem not their sin, their crime less deep
Because the evil that is done
Goes not into the street to weep.
Not less the trampled heart will bleed ;

THE FALLEN.

Not less will outraged feeling spurn
The venomed tongue whose envious greed
On all its blighting breath would turn,
Blind to all right where justice should discern.

These are the assassins of the heart;
No outward, open foe that scorn
Deceptions ways, the coward's part;
But lurking in the quiet morn
Of confidence, sow frightful tares
With hand so fair and purpose kind
That naught of its low object bares
To trusting, unsuspecting mind;
Yet what a harvest shall the future find!

Lone, barren hearts from which no more
Spring trust's sweet flowers that charm the sight,
But fade upon a hostile shore
Where every whisper in the night,
And each caress, is feignèd love

Schooled in deceit but to betray;
Ah, when I think that such should thrive,
Doubt will arise and question free:
Which are the fallen, which have strayed away?

And still they bow the knee to Baal,
With homage that a slave would spurn,
Nor ask will retribution fail
Secure upon the course they run.
O, wretched, self-deluded soul,
Still one tribunal yet remains—
The mind its terrors will unroll;
Remorse consume what malice gains,
And self-loathed life wreck envy's cherished fanes.

ALICE.

"I had rather live and love where Death is king, than have eternal life where love is not."

She's gone, they say, as some sweet flower
That made earth smile like Eden's bower,
   Till we forgot the winter's storm,
Forgot that grief, in one short hour,
   Could blast our hopes so fond and warm,
   And shroud in death that fairest form,
Not made for earth, but Heaven's dower.

O, who can tell what feelings rise,
What throes of grief, what yearning sighs
   With her dear name are breathed in vain?
What words can speak, what suppliant eyes
   Can half portray the minds long train
   Of hope and fear, of joy and pain?
The angels weep when nature dies.

We miss thee as the genial day—
When sunshine flooded all our way—
   That's followed by the icy storms
Of winter, night and gloom and gray;
   Whose influence no longer warms
   The apathy of our cold forms—
A warmth and beauty lost for aye.

The snow that falls upon thy mound,
And shrouds thy lovely image round,
   Is but an emblem of thy soul
In purity to softly bound.
   O, who could dream that fate would roll,
   With chilling hand from utmost pole,
Such floods of grief? All hopes are drowned.

For him to whom thy upward flight
Brings deepest care and lonely night,
   Our strongest sympathy is moved.
O, friend, good cheer; this sorrow's blight
   Time will atone, and she thou loved
   Will reappear to thee bereaved,
In those frail forms of love's young light.

And in their lives not long begun
There is a hope, a joy not won
    Unhedged by care, for here our lives
Find a soft echo, as the sun
    When faded in the west, still shines
    In the pale moon—one flower fades,
Another lovelier blooms again.

MEMORIAL DAY.

I strew no flowers upon the dead to-day;
Can human valor sink with human clay?
    Their deeds remain—all that they gave
    For liberty, no earthly grave
Confines or fetters, for the patriot soul
Surrendered not th' immortal with its dole.

And as the years go on, and History's tree
Spreads its broad limbs from gulf to either sea—
    And peopled millions fill the lands
    Now ravaged o'er by savage bands—
Each blow, each life that freedom's cause can claim,
Shall from the nation draw increasing fame.

MEMORIAL DAY.

The heart must hold the sacred memory,
Else rites prescribed are hollow mockery;
    No beauty lend nor lessons teach
    That will to future ages reach,
If minds ungrateful to the debt they owe,
Seek to dismiss it by a flaunting show.

And still, this outward homage that is given,
As long as tears from widowed eyes are driven,
    Cannot amiss be ever deemed;
    But truest honer never streamed
From martial drums and wreaths that quickly fade,
And festal garb that follows in parade.

This must not be; the nation that's reborn
From war's fierce womb, in conflict torn,
    Shall higher mount and place their names
    Beyond what chance and change assumes;
And Plymouth will with Jamestown then unite,
And Liberty build altars on each site.

I strew no flowers; the heart when feeling most
Would not its grief and reverence lightly boast
    In emblems that from custom start;
    And though this day be set apart,
It seems more fit for me, if in my song
I help one mind, aspiring, from the throng.

1885.

BYRON.

He touched his harp and nations heard, entranced.
— *Pollock.*

O, bard immortal, if thy ill-starred life
   Was not conformed to this most rigid world;
If thy impetuous soul was ever rife
   With warring doubts, daring to speak what hurl'd
   The malice of an envious time unfurl'd
Upon thy brow sublime, fair genius to enshrine
Her brightest gem—from country self-exiled,
   Wandering in every land—sought thee alone; ·
We can forgive thy faults, thy gifts so brightly shone.

Thine was a burning, ever restless spirit,
   Seeming as if Prometheus had inflamed
Thee, too, with heavenly fire, and boldly sent it
   Glowing through thy every line; and unreclaimed,
   The wild torents of thy soul—nor ever chained—

Burst forth from their deep source unceasingly.
Yet shall we look beyond thy life defamed;
   Beyond the clouds that hang so blightingly
Causing their gloom to gather o'er thy verse,
   Like some foreboding spectre, though unseen,
Sapping thy life, yet felt the doubly worse;—
   Justice will come and save thy honor's sheen.

Dying at last for liberty and right,
   Greece holds thee ever as her cherished son;
Though thy clay rests not on her ancient site—
   Nor monument points to the good there done,
   And the heroic spirit of the race is gone—
When freedom's name is whispered by the bold,
Thine shall have power, e'en as the dead of old.

BANQUET SONG.

Let the dear old time's we've spent
   Mid these honored halls,
Be recalled with glad content,
   As the lamp-light falls
Softly o'er this festive scene,
Filled with pleasure, joy serene.

Cho.—Hail, hail! This glad to-night!
   Let our hearts join with delight—
   Banquet, song and merriment—
   May long live this bright present.

Bacchus is our king to-night,
   God of mirth and song,
And we'll pledge with chalice bright,
   Friendship true and strong—
For these moments, n'er forgot,
Form of life its brightest spot.

Who shall quell this flowing tide?
   For our spirits free
Banish trouble, cares deride,
   Mid such company;
And again, with bursts of pleasure,
Rings our song of gayest measure.

May we often meet again
   In the bright To Be,
And recall with happy strain
   Days of thoughtless glee.
Yes, let friendship's goblet flow
With youth's purest, sweetest glow.

Pennsylvania College.

NORMIA.

How dare I call from out her home of light
The muse of song to grace this humble flight?
This simple tribute to a name unknown,
Save from the lips of those who spoke alone
The eulogy of tend'rest hope and praise,
  And came with willing feet to place with love
Their off'rings on the shrine of friendship's days,
  The last, but sad devotion life can prove.

A stranger's hand essays what friends would write,
And through the gloom and mystery and night,
That shrouds the form wrapped in eternal sleep,
Would send this little hope-song of the deep,
Nor silent sympathy he feels for all
On whom may rest the shadow of death's pall.
  The world's philosophy, the cynic's sneer,
Ne'er poured a balm upon the sorrowing heart,
  When all is lost that's held of earth most dear,
Nor caused from pity's eye a tear to start.

Perhaps he, too, had sorrows that the throng
Gazed on unmoved—shadows that linger long
Upon the sunlight and the joys of life—
But buried deep beneath the whirl and strife
Of worldly duty and the round of years,
That call for action, not ignoble tears;
   Yet they remain, and from the far-off past
Are ever wakened when the chords are touched,
   E'en by another's grief—such as this last—
That stirs the slumb'ring memory of the loved.

The warp and woof of life with shuttles swift,
Or slow with weary years that scarcely drift,
Weave a strange tapistry of gloom and glow;
There stand the three that watch its figures grow,
The dreaded Parcae, wrinkled, old and gray,
That clip the threads ere half is spun away.
   They heed not hope, nor youth, nor beauty, there,
The pictured scene though filled with rarest hue—
   What care they for the griefs we have to bear?—
Is stopped ere life with midway joy is due.

THANKSGIVING.

Thanksgiving! rings the welcome shout!
Joy to our nation! Far throughout
   Her utmost borders let it sound!
   Thanks to our God the nation's bound
In love again, nor war, nor doubt
   Bids justice, truth and right confound.

Let all the thousand birds that go
To tropic climes from realms of snow,
   Proclaim this message in their flight;
   The Lord is king and rules with might
Upon a princely throne below,
   Nor Liberty his altars slight.

An hundred years have sped away,
Of peace and wars in dark array,

But right still triumphs and more bright
Shines progress as our guiding light—
That flame which lights the world to-day,
Rose from our shoes, resplendent sight!

O, star of hope, to patriot heart!
Thy beams are fairer far that start
From Liberty's emblazoned crown,
Than Plead lustre of renown,
Or those that triple Orion impart,
Where southern skies their beauty own.

O, never may the ship of State
Be trusted to a hand which fate
Has formed unhallowed; never must
Her guidance fall to heart of lust,
Though mind of power and learning great
Would hold the helm of sacred trust.

THE FATE OF TASSO.

O, Italia, land of art and song!
  Home of the muses, in thy genial clime
  Apollo lingered with his harp sublime,
And taught great Dante there in numbers long—
To sing as that blind poet of the Isle—
  Of Hell in epic strain we love to trace;
  Tuned Petrarch's lyre love's purest theme to grace,
Rienzi's friend—Rome's tribune without guile.

To thee, O, Tasso, yet 'twas left to sing
  Of chivalry; Jerusalem Delivered;
  And as thy genius shone the age revered;
Wealth, royalty, the court, the haughty king,
Owned thy true worth and sought thee for their own;
  All heaped up honors, led thy ambition high;
  The end, to take thy freedom and deny
The fame thy pen so nobly won.

Deserted by the ones who praised thee most,
   The prison was thy doom, the grated cell;
   Thy crime, the glory known to ages well.
They thought by iron bars, that envious host,
To confine thy great soul within their gloom;
   To quinch the flame that shone upon the world
   In glowing strains; their coward malice hurled
When none were left to shield thee from that doom.

And thou, Alphonso, name linked with scorn,
   Thy heart was barred against his suppliant song,
   Nor touched by lines which told his cruel wrong,
But left him in his dungeon, sad, forlorn,
Until his mind was sickened and his fancy
   Grew dull and languid with long-wasting years;
   Till spirits visit his sweet dreams, all fears
Dispell, and hope returns to set him free.

And now, Ferrara, thou art desolate!
   Thy gorgeous palaces are in the dust;
   Thy splendor soon forgotten with the rust
Of time, thy beauty and thy power once great.

The wandering owl at eve with wailing cry,
   Perched on some broken wall, now hoots in scorn
   The folly of thy greatness, as to warn
The traveller from such baseless phantasy.

When these have faded with their pomp and pride
   From earth and memory, and their high lords
   Forgotten save in infamy, rewards
Will come to thee, O, bard, such as abide
All time and change, and know not dull decay
   While song and beauty hold a sacred place
   In our short lives, and those who trace
Thy work transcendent in a distant day.

Tasso, on thy laureate circled brow,
   The crown still blooming in its loveliness
   With fame's sweet flowers, thy wrongs would now
     redress—
The crown which none had worn through years till
     now,

Since Petrarch's song rang in the hearts of Italy;
   And while the jewels of *her* kingly crown
   Grow dim in ages hence, brighter renown
Thy simple wreath will gain, and immortality.

'Twas thy sad lot to love beyond thy reach,
   And waste away the years in hopeless passion;
   But not because she shunned thee; thou hadst won
Her deep regard; her rank had caused the breach,
And pride, such as high state to women gives,
   And battles with her love till it lies conquer'd;—
   Thy softest pleadings heeded not or heard,
But barred her breast 'gainst thee where nature strives.

The pilgrim to great genius' reverenced shrine
   When straying in the land thy glory famed,—
   Thy fate dishonored, yet its pride has claimed—
His tears with pity's off'ring will resign;
And feeling thy deep suffering, cruel shame,
   Will then exclaim: O, thou great Tasso! led
   By true ambition, the unhonored dead
Have sought in vain to blight thy growing fame.

www.ingramcontent.com/pod-product-compliance
Lightning Source LLC
Chambersburg PA
CBHW030251170426
43202CB00009B/708